A Note to Parents and Teachers

DK READERS is a compelling programme for beginning readers, designed in conjunction with literacy experts, including Maureen Fernandes, B.Ed (Hons). Maureen has spent many years teaching literacy, both in the classroom and as a specialist in schools.

Beautiful illustrations and superb full-colour photographs combine with engaging, easy-to-read text to offer a fresh approach to each subject in the series.

Each DK READER is guaranteed to capture a child's interest while developing his or her reading skills, general knowledge and love of reading.

The five levels of DK READERS are aimed at different reading abilities, enabling you to choose the books that are exactly right for your child:

Pre-level 1: Learning to read

Level 1: Beginning to read

Level 2: Beginning to read alone

Level 3: Reading alone

Level 4: Proficient readers

The 'normal' age at which a child begins to read can be anywhere from three to eight years old, so these levels are only a general guideline.

No matter which level you select, you can be sure that you are helping your child learn to read, then read to learn!

LONDON, NEW YORK, MUNICH,
MELBOURNE AND DELHI

Senior Editor Catherine Saunders
Designer Sandra Perry
Brand Manager Lisa Lanzarini
Publishing Manager Simon Beecroft
Category Publisher Alex Allan
Production Nick Seston

Reading Consultant
Maureen Fernandes

Lucasfilm Ltd.
Executive Editor Jonathan Rinzler
Art Director Troy Alders
Continuity Editor Leland Chee
Director of Publishing Carol Roeder

First published in Great Britain in 2008 by
Dorling Kindersley Limited,
80 Strand, London WC2R 0RL

6 8 10 9 7 5

020-SD350-Mar/2008

A CIP catalogue record for this book is available
from the British Library.

ISBN: 978-1-40532-937-8

Colour reproduction by GRB Editrice S.r.l., London
Printed and bound by L-Rex, China

Discover more at
www.dk.com

Contents

DK READERS

STAR WARS™
EPIC BATTLES

PROFICIENT
4
READERS

Written by Simon Beecroft

What side are you on?

Jedi Knights
The Jedi use a mysterious energy called the Force. Jedi Knights carry glowing lightsabres to defend themselves.

A long time ago, in a galaxy far, far away, a great and peaceful Republic existed. Each planet, large or small, made its voice heard in a huge Senate building on the capital planet, Coruscant. The Jedi Knights defended peace and justice everywhere. They ensured that arguments between planets were sorted out without violence or war.

Battle droids
The Trade Federation built many millions of machine-soldiers called battle droids. Each battle droid carries a deadly blaster weapon.

Sadly, this peace was about to be smashed. A greedy business organisation called the Trade Federation created an army and began to invade planets, starting with a small world called Naboo. As the conflict grew, the Republic later deployed its own army. With the galaxy at war, both sides learnt too late that they had been manipulated by a deadly Sith Lord!

Sith Lord
The Sith have deadly evil powers. The Sith Lord Darth Sidious plots to destroy the Jedi and rule the entire galaxy.

Warmongers
The Trade Federation and other greedy business corporations take orders from the Sith and use their droid armies to attack the Republic.

The Sith were the greediest beings in the galaxy. The leader was called Darth Sidious and he was secretly controlling the Trade Federation. He wanted it to start a war that would put him in power as Emperor. He fooled everyone by pretending to be a kindly politician called Senator Palpatine. Palpatine became leader of the Senate, took control of the Republic's army, and forced every planet to obey him.

Hired hands
Sith Lords often hire assassins, spies and bounty hunters to do their dirty work for them. Bounty hunters are skilled hunters who kidnap people for a fee.

A few brave people refused to accept Palpatine's evil Empire. They were called the Rebel Alliance – and they set out to free the galaxy.

This is the story of the Emperor's rise to power and his downfall at the hands of the brave-hearted Rebels. It is a story of great struggles on land and in space. From all-out attacks to deadly duels and fights with savage beasts, these battles are epic!

Rebels at the ready
Luke Skywalker, his twin sister Princess Leia, Han Solo and the Wookiee Chewbacca all fight for the Rebel Alliance.

Legendary land battles

Vile leaders
The Trade Federation's cowardly leaders land on Naboo only after their battle droids have captured the royal palace.

The galaxy first erupted into violence when the Trade Federation invaded Naboo. This peaceful planet was home to the Naboo people and a water-dwelling species called the Gungans. Two Jedi were sent to investigate: Qui-Gon Jinn and Obi-Wan Kenobi. With help from the Gungans, the Jedi rescued the Naboo Queen, Padmé Amidala.

The Jedi took Queen Amidala to Coruscant to ask the Senate for its help. But the Senate was all talk and no action. Amidala would have to free her planet herself!

She and the Jedi returned to Naboo and battled their way to the hangar where their spaceships were housed. Then Amidala led an attack on the royal palace, fighting many battle droids. Elsewhere, the Gungans fought a battle-droid army. Now the Naboo pilots had to destroy the Trade Federation ship that was controlling the battle droids.

Swift strike
Qui-Gon slices a deadly battle droid in two as he helps Queen Amidala escape from her planet.

Back-up droid
Droideka are even more deadly than battle droids. They carry twin blaster weapons.

Return to Naboo
Qui-Gon Jinn and Obi-Wan Kenobi lead the attempt to recapture Queen Amidala's palace.

The deadly land battle between the Gungan army and the massed ranks of battle droids took place on a wide-open grassy plain. At first the Gungans were very clever. They activated special machines carried by their giant swamp lizards. These machines generated an energy bubble that protected the Gungan army from high-speed airborne missiles.

Gungan soldiers face the might of the Trade Federation's droid army.

Boss Nass
Queen Amidala asks the Gungan ruler, Boss Nass, to help her fight the invaders.

But the Gungans did not realise that battle droids could walk right through their shield. Now the two armies battled each other inside the shield. The Gungans fought bravely but could not hope to win against an endless supply of battle droids. It would take a space battle above Naboo to shut down the droid army.

Binoculars

Atlatl

Electropole

War weapons
Gungans use a variety of unusual weapons that fire balls of explosive energy called plasma. They hurl these balls into the air with catapults and throwing sticks called atlatls.

Energy shields
Gungan soldiers carry glowing energy shields into battle to protect themselves from blaster bolts fired by battle droids.

New leader
The Neimoidian leaders are joined by a powerful new ally, the former Jedi, Count Dooku.

Wheel droids
Sinister hailfire droids roll into battle on giant hoop wheels, while Republic gunships prepare to strike from above.

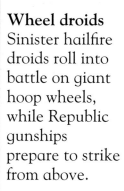

After the Republic learnt that its enemies were creating huge droid armies, it was tricked into using a ready-made army to defend itself. Its Army consisted of millions of clone troopers – each clone was an identical copy of a single ultimate soldier. This hastily assembled army first saw action on a planet called Geonosis.

Jedi generals
At the battle of Geonosis, Yoda and many other Jedi have to become military generals for the first time.

Advance guard
Clone troopers blast their way toward the enemy, using special sight systems in their helmets to see through the dense smoke on the battlefield.

The droid armies attacked the Jedi in a large arena on Geonosis. When clone troopers joined the fray, led by Jedi Master Yoda, the battle spread outside the arena. Many Jedi and clone troopers were killed, but finally the droids and their masters retreated. This was the first battle of the famous Clone Wars.

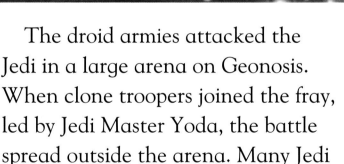

Tarfful
One of the
Wookiee leaders
is called Tarfful.
When the
Republic's clone
troopers,
wheeled tanks
and walking
guns go into
battle against
the droids,
Tarfful and
the Wookiees
are right
alongside them.

Droid armies
attacked everywhere.
One of the biggest battles
took place on Kashyyyk. This
planet was home to tall, furry
creatures called Wookiees. The
Wookiees and the Republic army
fought on land and sea. But just as
victory was in sight, it all went
wrong. The Republic did not know
that their clone troopers had been
brainwashed to switch sides when
they received a special signal.

Tanks roll in
On Kashyyyk, many Trade Federation tanks roll over land and water with battle droids mounted on the sides.

When the clones received the signal, Order 66, they turned their weapons on their Jedi generals. The clones took orders only from the Sith. When Darth Sidious became Emperor, the clone troopers became his personal army, known now as stormtroopers. The Empire was born.

Assassination
When the Sith signal is received, every clone commander turns on the Jedi. Nearly all the Jedi leaders are killed. Aayla Secura is assassinated while fighting on the fungi planet, Felucia.

Walking tanks
The Empire's terrifying walking tanks, called AT-ATs, advance across the snow toward the Rebel base.

Great land battles took place in the time of the Empire, too. Many brave individuals joined the Rebel Alliance and fought against the Empire, though they had few weapons, vehicles, or other resources. The Emperor and Darth Vader put much of the Empire's military might toward crushing the Rebel Alliance.

Front line
The Rebels try to hold off the advancing AT-ATs with their heavy guns.

Rebel hangar
The Rebel base is a converted ice cave, with a massive hangar for vehicles.

Darth Vader discovered that the Rebels had built a secret base on the ice planet Hoth. His troops attacked it with great force. He sent in giant walking tanks called AT-ATs. The Rebels tried to hold off the AT-ATs for as long as they could, and even managed to destroy two of them. But eventually they were forced to flee and find another hiding place.

Enter Vader
Sith Lord Darth Vader enters the Rebel base, which is now a smoking ruin. He is flanked by stormtroopers equipped for missions in sub-zero conditions.

Scout trooper
Imperial scout
troopers on
flying speeder
bikes chase
down the Rebels
when they land
on Endor.

After the defeat at Hoth, the Rebels hid all over the galaxy. Palpatine hatched a plan to draw them out. He had once built a huge super-weapon called the Death Star, which the Rebels had destroyed. Now he built a second Death Star, knowing the Rebels would try to stop him. Then he would blow the Rebel fleet out of the sky.

Battle in the forest
Stormtroopers, backed up by a walking AT-ST cannon, do battle with Han and Chewbacca.

The Death Star was protected by a shield generator on the forest moon of Endor. A team of Rebels led by Luke Skywalker, Princess Leia, Han Solo and Chewbacca went to Endor to destroy the generator. The Rebels faced a large Imperial army, but they were helped by natives called Ewoks. Together they suceeded in destroying the shield generator, and then the Rebel fleet was able to attack the Death Star.

Ewok attack
Small, determined Ewoks hurl rocks at stormtroopers in their well-planned attacks.

Rebel team
Han tries to break into the generator bunker while Leia holds off advancing stormtroopers.

Space battles

Many of the biggest battles in the galaxy took place in space. When the Trade Federation invaded Naboo, its massive battleships surrounded the planet. While the conflict raged on the ground, a handful of Naboo ships managed to take off and fly towards the battleships.

Feared fleet
Deadly Trade Federation vulture droid ships emerge from the ring-shaped Droid Control Ship.

Rookie pilot
Anakin is whisked into the space battle when the autopilot engages in the starfighter he is hiding in.

One of the Naboo ships was flown – at first, accidentally – by a nine-year-old boy called Anakin Skywalker. Anakin had Jedi abilities and was a superb pilot, although he had never flown a starship before. He managed to enter the Trade Federation's Droid Control Ship and fire torpedoes into its reactor room, escaping in his starfighter as the ship exploded. Anakin's incredible feat saved Naboo.

Brave strike
Starfighters avoid deadly laser blasts.

Blown away
The Control Ship sends instructions to every battle droid. When it is destroyed, the droids stop fighting.

Close combat
A Naboo starfighter narrowly avoids a direct hit as the Droid Control Ship fires at oncoming Naboo ships.

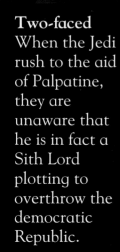

Jedi team
Anakin and Obi-Wan fly side-by-side in their fast Interceptors.

The space battle above Naboo was just the beginning. Worse was yet to come. A full-scale war broke out between the Republic and the droid armies. Their battle fleets met in a gigantic space conflict above Coruscant. The leader of the Republic, Supreme Chancellor Palpatine, had been kidnapped, and two Jedi set off to rescue him: Obi-Wan Kenobi and Anakin Skywalker.

Two-faced
When the Jedi rush to the aid of Palpatine, they are unaware that he is in fact a Sith Lord plotting to overthrow the democratic Republic.

Direct hit
Both sides lose some of their spaceships in the explosive space battle above Coruscant.

The Jedi dodged enemy fire and landed on the cruiser in which Palpatine was being held. After freeing Palpatine, Anakin had to pilot the cruiser to a crash landing after a Republic ship tore it apart.

Tiny but deadly
Small buzz droids attach themselves to the side of Obi-Wan's ship to inflict damage with their cutting arms.

Deadly sky
Republic warships engage droid fighters large and small in the raging battle above Coruscant.

Some space battles involved many ships, like the battle above Coruscant. In others, just two ships engaged in a duel called a dogfight. When Obi-Wan was on the trail of a dangerous villain called Jango Fett, the chase led into a highly lethal asteroid field. Any collision with these floating rocks would be fatal. Jango tried to lose Obi-Wan by blasting rocks close to the Jedi's ship.

Distinctive ship
Jango pilots one of the deadliest ships in the galaxy, *Slave I*. It is armed with weapons and lethal surprises.

Young ally
Jango Fett's son, Boba, travels in *Slave I* with his father, learning from his every action.

Obi-Wan was a skilled pilot and he dodged each explosion. Then Jango steered his ship around an asteroid so he was now the one pursuing Obi-Wan. He fired a special seeker missile, but Obi-Wan faked his ship's explosion. When Jango saw the blast, he believed that Obi-Wan had been killed, but the clever Jedi was really hiding on one of the asteroids.

On the tail
Seeker missiles can home in on fast-moving objects so they are hard to shake off.

Jedi pilot
Even though Obi-Wan says he is not keen on flying, his piloting skills are superb.

Trusty ship
The *Falcon* is battle scarred from its many space adventures.

Another ship that has been in many dogfights is the *Millennium Falcon*. Piloted by Han Solo and Chewbacca, the ship could outrun most enemy craft. If the going got tough, the *Falcon* could jump to lightspeed, enabling it to vanish instantly and reappear somewhere far away.

Under pressure
A giant Star Destroyer chases the *Falcon* while Imperial TIE-fighters blast it with laser fire.

Han Solo flew the *Falcon* in many
daring raids against the Imperial
fleet. Once, he landed right on the
hull of an enormous Imperial Star
Destroyer to evade its radar.
Another time, he made the
seemingly suicidal decision
to fly into an asteroid
field to shake off Imperial
fighters. The daring plan
worked and he escaped
with his life.

Rebel space battles

Death Star
The moon-sized Death Star had the firepower to destroy an entire planet.

Strike force
Rebel teams of X-wing and Y-wing starfighter pilots fly from their base on Yavin 4 towards the Death Star.

The Rebel Alliance was dedicated to opposing the oppressive rule of the Empire, despite being desperately under-equipped. The Empire had a massive starfleet, but the Alliance made do with a small number of battle-worn starfighters.

The Alliance learnt that the Empire had built an enormous battle station called the Death Star. Stolen plans showed a flaw: If a Rebel starfighter could fire a torpedo into a tiny exhaust port, the chain reaction would destroy the battle station.

Rebel pilot
Luke stays calm and focused in his starfighter spaceship as he leads the attack on the Death Star.

The Rebel pilots boldly launched an assault on the Death Star from their base on the planet Yavin 4. The Empire was not expecting an attack on its deadly superweapon. One Rebel pilot was skilled enough to strike the target: Luke Skywalker. The Death Star exploded – and the Rebels scored their first major victory against the Empire.

Enemy ships
Two Imperial ships chase the Rebel pilots along a narrow trench on the Death Star.

Hot shot
Luke hits the exhaust port that leads into the heart of the battle station's colossal reactor.

Rebel leader
Admiral Ackbar is the loyal Commander of the Rebel fleet at the Battle of Endor.

The battle rages around the half-completed Death Star.

The Battle of Endor was the final showdown between the Rebels and the Empire. Part of the conflict took place above the forest moon of Endor, where the Empire was building a second Death Star. While a team of Rebels landed on Endor's moon to disable the shield generator protecting the Death Star, the entire Rebel fleet came out of hiding to launch a final, do-or-die attack.

A Rebel ship crashes into the bridge of an Imperial Star Destroyer, while Rebel B-wings fly in formation nearby.

At one point in the battle, Rebels targeted the Empire's Star Destroyers, hoping the Death Star would hold fire to avoid hitting its own ships. The battle turned when a damaged Rebel ship crashed into a Super Star Destroyer. With the shield down, Rebel ships could attack the Death Star's power plant, causing a fatal explosion.

Direct assault
The *Millennium Falcon* flew through the Death Star's superstructure to detonate the battle station's power plant.

Lightsabre clashes

Since ancient times, the lightsabre has been the chosen weapon of the Jedi Knights. Until the Sith emerged from hiding, the Jedi used their lightsabres only as defence against blasters and other weapons. But the Sith also used lightsabres. Now the Jedi faced opponents armed with their own traditional weapon.

Surprise attack
Darth Maul first appears on the desert planet Tatooine. He ambushes Jedi Qui-Gon Jinn.

Sith opponent
On Naboo, it takes two skilled Jedi to hold back Darth Maul's double-bladed lightsabre.

Obi-Wan leaps to avoid a low parry from Maul's glowing blade.

Final strike
Qui-Gon meets Maul in a clash that would spell the Jedi's doom.

Jedi in trouble
On the edge of a deep shaft, Maul nearly triumphs over Obi-Wan. But the Jedi will not give up until he has defeated the savage Sith.

During the Battle of Naboo, Darth Sidious's Sith apprentice, Darth Maul, emerged. Maul's appearance was terrifying, with face tattoos, yellow eyes and several horns. Darth Maul attacked Jedi Qui-Gon Jinn and Obi-Wan Kenobi. He managed to kill Qui-Gon. Obi-Wan was devastated but he fought on until he had defeated his Sith foe.

Sith blade
Dooku's lightsabre blade is red, as all Sith blades are.

Captured Jedi
On Geonosis, Count Dooku wants Obi-Wan Kenobi to join him as a Sith.

With Darth Maul dead, Sith Lord Darth Sidious had to train a new apprentice. He chose a former Jedi called Count Dooku. The elegant, commanding Dooku left the Jedi Order to become a Sith. Sidious taught him to use the destructive dark side of the Force.

At the Battle of Geonosis, Dooku fought a great Jedi Master, Yoda. They clashed in a blur of lightsabre blows. Dooku used the Force to throw massive objects. This time, he managed to escape.

Jedi against Sith
The Jedi fight Dooku
on board the cruiser.

Dooku next
faced Obi-Wan
and Anakin on
the cruiser where
Palpatine (really Darth
Sidious) was being held prisoner.
Dooku knocked Obi-Wan
unconscious. But he was unaware of
Sidious's masterplan: he wanted
Anakin to kill Dooku and replace
him as his new Sith apprentice.

Bad influence
Palpatine
encourages
Anakin to reject
his Jedi training
and unleash his
anger to kill
Dooku in
cold blood.

Count Dooku was not the only lightsabre-wielding foe the Jedi would meet during the Clone Wars. They also confronted a half-machine, half-living creature called Grievous, who was general of the droid armies. Grievous had also been trained by Count Dooku in lightsabre combat. He liked to steal lightsabres from the Jedi he killed, and hoped to add Obi-Wan and Anakin's weapons to his collection.

Lethal general
On Utapau, Obi-Wan finds that General Grievous is a dangerous opponent in lightsabre combat.

Utapau chase
Grievous on his wheelbike and Obi-Wan on a fast varactyl lizard trade blows on the planet Utapau.

Furious foe
Grievous's arms can split into four, giving the Jedi extra lightsabres to dodge and parry. Obi-Wan will shear off some of these extra limbs.

But not this time! The daring Jedi fought off Grievous's bodyguards and escaped the general's clutches.

Grievous next met Obi-Wan on the planet Utapau. Wielding four lightsabres, Grievous unleashed a brutal assault. A high-speed chase led to a final showdown – and Grievous's dramatic demise in an exploding ball of fire.

Explosive end
Obi-Wan uses a blaster to fire the fatal shots that enflame Grievous.

Lost cause
On the volcano planet called Mustafar, Obi-Wan realises that Anakin is no longer a Jedi.

Sith opponent
Anakin, now called Darth Vader, unleashes his Sith powers against Obi-Wan Kenobi.

Ever since Senator Palpatine first met Anakin Skywalker, he knew the young Jedi had great powers. He also perceived Anakin's unruly emotions and knew he could be turned to the Sith cause. After he had encouraged Anakin to kill Dooku, Palpatine revealed that he was a Sith, and Anakin joined him, becoming Darth Vader. Then Palpatine made Vader believe Obi-Wan was against him.

Anakin's eyes gleam with anger as Obi-Wan defeats him in battle.

Darth Vader and Obi-Wan fought on the volcano planet Mustafar. Obi-Wan gained the upper hand and left Vader for dead. But Emperor Palpatine rebuilt Vader in black armour. Then Vader took his place beside the Emperor.

Darth Vader fought Obi-Wan once more, taking the Jedi's life. It wasn't until he battled with his own son that Vader was able to reject the Sith and the dark side.

Deadly rematch
Vader and Obi-Wan meet in combat for the last time on the first Death Star.

Father-son duel
Vader wants his son Luke to join him as a Sith, but Luke refused.

Cruel Master
Palpatine enjoys the fight between his Sith accomplice, Dooku and his accomplice-to-be, Anakin.

Sith unmasked
Palpatine displays his Sith lightsabre skills in the fight with Mace Windu.

For a long time, the most evil Sith Lord in the galaxy went by the name of Palpatine. Pretending to be a friend to the Republic, he secretly masterminded a war that made him the cruel ruler of the galaxy.

The Jedi realised too late that Palpatine was really a Sith Lord called Darth Sidious. High-ranking Jedi Master Mace Windu lost his life attempting to stop the Sith schemer.

Palpatine had hidden his Sith lightsabre until Mace confronted him.

Even Yoda was unable to defeat the Emperor in lightsabre combat. In the end, Sidious's own ally, Darth Vader, sided with Vader's son, Luke Skywalker. Vader turned against his Sith Master and threw Emperor Palpatine to his death.

Explosive clash
The two most powerful users of the Force's light and dark sides clash in a spectacular duel in the Senate building on Coruscant.

Lightning strike
Sidious fires deadly Sith lightning at Luke. But Vader will be unable to stand by and let his son die.

Famous showdowns

Jango finds that Obi-Wan is hard to hit with a blaster.

Airborne foe
Jango uses his jetpack to soar above Obi-Wan on Kamino.

Final end
In the arena battle on Geonosis, Jedi Mace Windu strikes the fatal blow that ends Jango's life.

Even before the Clone Wars, the galaxy was not entirely peaceful. Many criminals thrived, including bounty hunters, who captured or attacked people for a price. The best bounty hunter in the galaxy was called Jango Fett. Jango wore sleek armour and carried many weapons. He clashed with Obi-Wan on a watery planet called Kamino.

Though Jango escaped, the Battle of Geonosis would be his undoing. In the combat, Mace Windu struck Jango down with a powerful thrust from his lightsabre blade.

Jango's son Boba witnessed his father's death. Boba became a bounty hunter like his father. He came to work for Darth Vader and the notorious gangster Jabba the Hutt, among others. With Vader's help, Boba captured Han Solo and delivererd him to Jabba, who wanted Han for unpaid debts. A fierce battle ensued when Luke Skywalker and his friends rescued Solo from Jabba.

Battle-scarred
Boba Fett had many famous showdowns in his career as a bounty hunter. But he meets his match in the battle at Jabba's palace.

Deadly duel
Boba clashes with Luke, but a lucky strike from Han will knock the bounty hunter out of the battle.

Enter the beast
The three-horned reek enters the arena on Geonosis for a showdown with the human prisoners.

Jedi Knights, Rebels and other defenders of freedom in the galaxy have had many showdowns with bounty hunters, assassins and vile gangsters. They have also faced some nightmarish beasts.

On the planet Geonosis, Obi-Wan, Anakin and Padmé Amidala were sentenced to public execution – by savage beasts.

Bared teeth
A soldier prods the nexu into the arena with a spear, where it bears its fangs in anticipation of fresh meat.

Obi-Wan faces the fearsome acklay in the Geonosis arena.

The blood-thirsty acklay walked on three pairs of giant claws. The reek had three pointed horns on its head for goring opponents. The nexu had a mouthful of sharp teeth. Obi-Wan managed to fell the acklay with his lightsabre blade. Anakin jumped on top of the reek and charged it into the nexu.

Rancor beast
In Jabba's palace, a caged beast called a rancor is let loose upon Luke Skywalker, but proves no match for the new Jedi.

Jabba's death
The massive slug-like gangster Jabba the Hutt meets an untimely end at the hands of Princess Leia.

45

A new era

At last – victory for the Rebel Alliance! The deaths of Emperor Palpatine and Darth Vader, and the destruction of the second Death Star, meant that the Empire was doomed. Peace and justice would soon be restored to the galaxy. The good news spread quickly and people rejoiced.

Father and son reunited
Luke looks at his father's true face for the first time, revealed beneath Darth Vader's helmet.

Forest celebration
In Endor's forests, Rebels and Ewoks celebrate the destruction of the terrible second Death Star that had threatened all of their lives.

The Rebel Alliance established a New Republic to replace the Empire. But troubles continued. Hundreds of planets that had accepted the Emperor's rule needed to be won over. Many loyal Imperial officers continued to attack the New Republic with remnants of the Imperial fleet. For Luke Skywalker, Han Solo, Princess Leia and their allies, a new era had begun but the epic battle was not over yet.

Good times
Above the gigantic skyscrapers on Coruscant, fireworks light up the skies in celebration of the defeat of the evil Empire.

Glossary

Alien
A creature from outer space.

Apprentice
A person who is learning a skill.

Asteroid
A rock that floats in space.

Blaster
A gun that fires a deadly beam of light.

Clone
An exact copy of another person.

Dark side
The part of the Force associated with hatred.

Death Star
A moon-sized superweapon developed by the Empire.

Emperor
The leader of an Empire is called an Emperor. Palpatine is the Emperor who rules the Galactic Empire.

Empire
A group of peoples ruled by one leader.

The Force
An energy field created by all living things.

Force lightning
A Sith power, which involves firing deadly electricity from fingertips.

Galaxy
A group of millions of stars and planets.

Jedi Knight
A *Star Wars* warrior with special powers who defends the good of the galaxy.

Jedi Master
A high-ranking Jedi who has exceptional skills in using the Force.

Jedi Order
The name of the group that defends peace and justice in the galaxy.

Lightsabre
A Jedi's or Sith's sword-like weapon, with a blade of glowing energy.

Light side
The part of the Force associated with goodness, compassion and healing.

Lightspeed
A special kind of travel that allows a spaceship to cross vast distances of space in an instant.

Parry
To ward off a strike from a lightsabre or other sword-like weapon.

Reactor
A device in spaceships used to generate power for travel.

Rebel
Someone who opposes their government or ruler.

Republic
A nation or group of nations in which the people vote for their leaders.

Senate
The governing body of the Republic.

Senator
A member of the Senate. He or she will have been chosen (elected) by the people of his or her country.

Shield
An invisible protective barrier around a spaceship, planet or other object.

Sith
Enemies of the Jedi who use the dark side of the Force.